# Star Boy

*poems by*

# Paula Sergi

*Finishing Line Press*
Georgetown, Kentucky

# Star Boy

*This book is dedicated to those struggling with addiction and the people who love them.*

Copyright © 2021 by Paula Sergi
ISBN 978-1-64662-646-5 First Edition
All rights reserved under International and Pan-American Copyright Conventions. No part of this book may be reproduced in any manner whatsoever without written permission from the publisher, except in the case of brief quotations embodied in critical articles and reviews.

## ACKNOWLEDGMENTS

"Art and Science"—*verse-virtual.com*

"Bad Luck Head"—*The Village Pariah*

"Catch and Release"—*Manzanita*

"Crumbs" and "Dime at the Bottom of a Pocket"—*Family Business*—Finishing Line Press

Elegy for My Son's Abandoned Music Career"—*Grit, Gravity and Grace: New Poems About Health Care*—College of Physicians of Philadelphia

"Family Night at Rehab," "Scenes from an American Drama" and "The Road Finally Taken"—*SANA: Self Achievement through Nursing Art*, Fairfield University Egan

"Metamorphic" and "Star Boy Hears a Song"—*Terrain.org*

"Orbit"—*Cincinnati Review*

"Satellites"—*Sows Ear Poetry Review*

"Sherpa"—*Forgotten Women—A Tribute in Poetry*—Grayson Press

"Still Life with Plate of Pinecone or Fish"—*All We Can Hold: A Collection of Poetry on Motherhood*—Sage Hill Press

Publisher: Leah Huete de Maines
Editor: Christen Kincaid
Cover Art: Juliane Liebermann via Unsplash
Author Photo: Michael Sergi
Cover Design: Carolyn Adkins

Order online: www.finishinglinepress.com
also available on amazon.com

Author inquiries and mail orders:
Finishing Line Press
PO Box 1626
Georgetown, Kentucky 40324
USA

# Table of Contents

## Section 1
This is How it Started ... 1
Study: First Photo ... 2
Thirst ... 3
Dime at the Bottom of a Pocket ... 4
First Tracing ... 5
Metamorphic ... 6
Orbit ... 7
Art and Science ... 8
Catch and Release ... 9
Lift-off ... 10

## Section 2
Satellites ... 11
Fracture ... 12
Star Boy Hears a Song ... 13
Bad Luck Head ... 14
Exchange ... 15
Come to the Table ... 16
Sherpa ... 17
Still Life with Plate of Pinecone or Fish ... 18
Family Night at Rehab ... 19
Elegy for my Son's Abandoned Music Career ... 20

## Section 3
Scenes from an American Drama ... 21
E Mail Message ... 25
Mrs. Stoney's Journal ... 26
Another Family Night ... 27
Welcome to the ER ... 28
Rock Bottom ... 29
All Rise ... 30

## Epilogue
The Road Finally Taken ... 31
Crumbs ... 32
Asteroid ... 33
Zenith ... 34
Viento ... 35

*Often a star*
*waited for you to espy it and sense its light.*
*A wave rolled toward you out of the distant past,*
*or as you walked below an open window,*
*a violin gave itself to your hearing.*
                              Rainer Maria Rilke (second elegy)

# Section 1

### This is How it Started

Hard labor I expected, the crush
of ancient glaciers brought on by
my cravings for spicy kim chi
and a secret bag of Cheetos under my bed,
watched and waited for the brine,
his own small sea of comfort to appear.
Instead, he moved an elbow, fluttered
his long-lashed eyelids, curled his perfect toes,
sending blood trickling down my legs.
There should've been an ambulance.
Instead, his father insisted on driving
over roadways of packed snow,
over silent frozen rivers
where fish agree to keep breathing.
They cut a smile over my belly
and lifted him to the light
(though it was fluorescent, I'm sorry).
Perhaps he saw stars
and cried at such beauty
while I slept the false sleep of anesthesia.
Someone wiped him dry. Somewhere angels
sang a song I can't remember, the words obscure.
Then it was quiet and I wanted to memorize
each snowflake falling outside my window.

## Study: First Photo

Tufted hair flames
from his bullet shaped head,
an auburn turnip cap.
On the grey-green screen
of his heavy-lidded eyes
runs a film loop, a plot to rehearse.
His fists insist on clutching damp lint,
something for him to hang on to.
He is all folds and body fat,
jellied reserves for the lean years ahead.
His fleshy red lips blistered
by the first hot hit of my milk.

**Thirst**

He wants another glass of juice
but I say no. My words evaporate
before they reach his ears.
He looks past me to the patio
where pine siskins eat
at clear cylindrical feeders.

Hummingbirds gather,
sometimes crowd to drink
their red syrup, wings and tongues
moving faster than we can see.
They can have as much as they want
but have to fight for it.

One died last week.
He kept it in plastic, saved it
in an old bread bag
to show me the tongue,
how it really is translucent
and bifid, like the bird book says.

Paused in death, the only way
he'd ever see that tongue,
the only way he'd know,
for sure, about something
otherwise moving too fast
even for a young boy's eye.

## Dime at the Bottom of a Pocket

He wants to throw a penny into the fountain,
make a wish. Sluggish gold fish disconnect

in refracted underwater light
running out of oxygen.

He wants to swim all night
in the hotel pool, to dive for toys

on the bottom. There are rules,
I insist, and besides I'm too tired

to swim past eight. But I find a dime
at the bottom of a pocket for the fountain.

One underwater bulb has faded in
murky fountain water. He can't see

the coin land, heads or tails. Plastic
water lilies bounce with the coin's ripple

but don't move towards anything.
He wants to try again. When he looks

down for his luck, the hair in the valley
of his neck moves like caterpillars.

Sooner or later, it doesn't matter,
we're going to run out of change.

But here's a dime. Your last chance.
Don't ask again.

**First Tracing**

They traced their third grade bodies,
science on butcher paper, penciled outline.
Every time his partner's hand would rest
he punched a hole with lead.
His head looked too large,
his feet too small to walk on.
This is where your heart would be,
the teacher said, pointing somewhere

he didn't see, because the pattern
of punch holes was distracting.
They rolled the bodies to take home.
That's when he felt power the first time,
each star bursting through,
forming his own constellation,
a pattern he could follow
dot to dot.

**Metamorphic**

Star Boy believes that rocks are hardened stardust,
rejects the normal rock formation lore,
except *metamorphic* for the sound,
and how this rock became another kind.
How does one *morph*
he asks his mom. She doesn't understand,
talks about how boys grow up
to become men. He wants
to change his name to *metamorphic*,
because *asteroid* sounds girly and
then people could call him *morph* or *tam*
for short. Never mind, *tam* sounds girly,
and *Morph* too much like *Mort*,
an old-fashioned name that
someone's grandpa has. He could grow
into that like clothes that are too big
but doesn't want to. Last year
he wanted *Tyler*, like the boy who sat
behind him, but he moved away.
*Skylar* sounds close to the stars
or to the sky but that's a girl, again.
He's made an expedition to the creek
for stones and leaves them on his way
to school in case he can't remember
his way home —which is ridiculous
he knows —but fun, imagines holding part
of the sky in his hands, once they are bigger.

**Orbit**

At twelve, too old for carousels,
the horses fake and painted,
the lights electric, not
reflections from the sun
but if you squint, you can see stars
and if you knock your head hard
on the churning bars as you dismount
there would be stars, not
like you'd imagine, perfect
five point pattern, but stars of a kind
and if you did ride, succumbing
to the rise and fall, your horse
would be too tame despite its flashing teeth,
too white, and the disapproving adults
would appear every time around,
their faces knotted blurs
as if one orbit you'd break free
and take the horses with you.

**Art and Science**

He wanted to draw the star pattern
shaped like him. He'd add a ball
balancing off one toe, call it Star Boy.
The hills in his picture were purple,
like the way they really look.
But the teacher said no, hills are green,
you know this by middle school.
She said hold your paper parallel,
cut shapes like this. Said you aren't listening,
said I'm calling your mother,
quit doodling those stars,
how'd you like a referral,
boys are not really stars,
stars are not really boys,
said who do you think
you are? Brown hair, brown eyes.
Draw that. He sketched his constellation,
the one he first saw in third grade
and now it arranged itself easily
the way sugar crystals flicker in the blue
enamel bowl where birthday cakes
got started. And that color he made up
but later found on a chart
across from orange, labeled *royal*.
He thought about blue satin and
the shirt in the paint by number picture
over grandmother's dusty mantle where
the boy wore a hat with a feather
and held his rabbit still, how
the rabbit looked real, the boy scared,
misplaced, his half smile hiding a moustache
or mistaken brushstroke, shadow in bad light.
He felt his own upper lip, still bare,
remembered how the rabbit looked just right.

## Catch and Release

This lake was formed by glaciers,
sharp cut of ice against rock, scraping
everything in its path.
The water's odd edges form
a rough circumference fringed by leaf patterns,
each one waving like a green paper hand
on a cut-out chain from kindergarten.
My son invites me to join him—surprise number one—
on the paddle boat. Half way across he notices
I'm peddling fast, and he sees,
as if for the first time, that his mother has legs.
I remember the day we found tadpoles
along the drying creek bed, how he took them to school
in a jar. He says I need a shave and I tell him
once again about my summer in Alaska, long ago,
when I stopped shaving all together,
and that maybe this is the year
I give it up again.
That disgusts him, almost as much as touching
fish guts. But the lure of silver bass
is strong. He casts and the muscles of his back
ripple bronze and certain.
When his line goes taut, he yanks
and reels one in, but can't release the hook.
I look away, unable to face
the red facts of their gills.
*C'mon, hold still*, he says to the bass.
*I want to let you go.*
I think about my silver bracelet
with the broken latch,
I think I've found a metaphor, but really
it slipped from my wrist without my knowing.
And the aqua face of the lake flattens
when we turn to clear the sedgeweed at the sandbed.
A boat, a boy, a lake that holds us
above the sludge of prehistoric bones,
above all the trinkets lost
to over-eager fish, to fisherboys who reel too soon,
and those who turn away
out of fear for the mess,
the silver slice from a misled hook.

**Lift-off**

Imagine that moment of suspension
between here and …no special
destination. He wanted to fly—
not all the way to the North star
like the native boy he read about,
not to become a morning star.
Nor did he favor the life of an android boy
who lived in the future. This boy desired

to be gone from home.
Walking was too slow.
As there was no place to go,
there was no reason to jump a train,
though he enjoyed the tracks
for their message.

He was discouraged from sitting
on the roof of the house, from the oak's
highest branches. He had no wish
to jump. He couldn't admit
it was more about the bunny
in the baby bedtime books
his mother used to read, not just
the pictures, but how that bunny
wanted out, a little trip to get away
from home. The skateboard
was the perfect skiff,
lift-off, and that gift of air, never mind
the certain crash and fall.

# Section 2

## Satellites

The breeze this afternoon so self-assured
it doesn't have to raise its voice.

Star Boy cracks a skateboard
up and down the street,

spins the thin platform, and still standing,
lands on his feet. Body heat weaves

through his camouflage pants,
hisses through his pores.

Then he juggles a ball on the grass.
How many times can he lose it

from the toe of his shoe
and get it back?

We don't notice the earth's gentle tug,
how we're leaning towards the sun.

These summer days will drop
like amber beads from a frayed necklace.

We could live this way two, maybe
three more years. Maybe all afternoon.

**Fracture**

When his classmates traced his little boy
body in third grade science,
lumpy scars and mismatched bones
                rose from the butcher
paper X Ray, crayola'd purple and blue,
a public display of displaced joints.
But it didn't show the carnage
                yet to come; fractured
vertebrae, displaced thumb, sprains
and separations. Stitches. Broken nose.
Cleat marks on his cheek.
            He's designed his own
rite of puberty, as if to disengage
from the body I created, as if I cursed him
with his uncle's name.
                He emerges from the E.R.
swaddled in white harness and sling,
the nurse holding the skateboard.
This wasn't the parenthood I dreamed of
                those nine months of fantasy,
grace period before sin, original or otherwise
stained the yellow embryonic sac.
I imagined hopscotch and jump rope, chalk
                on our even-surfaced sidewalk,
kick the can or foursquare, never thought
he'd hurl himself over every edge,
or try *no hands* before he learned to steer.
                Step on a crack—please,
he doesn't have to break me.
It's just a chant designed
to teach restraint.

**Star Boy Hears a Song**

Maybe it's the woodchuck
on his way across the deck
his claws click clicking

or the gray squirrel overhead
on the airing porch gathering
nuts and dropping them in rhythm.

Maybe it's the downy
tapping on the maple's
one dead arm.

Maybe it's the neighbor's
garage door grinding out that tune
as it rises and falls,

another sound he can't explain,
a rabbit caught at night out back,
the snapping of a chicken neck,

the music they call rock
as if an asteroid landed on the lawn
and spun itself thin, a compact disc,

gears out of tune, sound out of time,
like railroad humming, passing cars,
clamber of Orion's falling sword

through earth's trees, lopping branches,
shouting *Timber*, stacking drumsticks,
notes piled outside Star Boy's window.

## Bad Luck Head

He used to have a secret garden
out back of the house
where the spring creek rush left
a brown patch of mud that never grew much,
and he imagined he alone might find there
what was left of summer, of childhood.
Cloudy, so he couldn't see which phase
of the moon he was under.
He could see illuminated numbers on his cell.
He dialed, dialed again but no one answered
so he walked. Dusk, the danger time
they said in driver's ed.
From outside looking in he saw
newscasters blaring silent predictions,
the adults all caged. Around the block
and further on where the streets went narrow,
he could feel the geese complaining
along their dark vee overhead.
The street lamp's fluorescent blink
winked at a gutter's damp clump,
not the carcass of someone's missing cat,
but a pumpkin crushed like a driver
in the evening news,
someone's bad luck head spilling
secret seeds that felt, in his hands,
like flattened stars,
still cold in their silky strands.

**Exchange**

Now that the double ruckus is over
I'd like to trade in Christmas and New Year's,
the ill-fitting sweater too long
in the sleeves, too tight around the waist,
and the pricey last-minute necklace,
a choker in rainbow colors,
trade in my hopes, already over-ruled,
for a holiday away from home,
an escape to cabin or hotel or condo,
someone's empty time share get-away,
bad carpet or not, fake fireplace or real,
pass on the paper plates of afternoon brunches,
cheesy potatoes and ham, the wan smiles
of friends' friends and relatives, avoid
their spectacle of scented candle exchange,
delete the image of our son falling
into glass shelving at the final open house
and the scuffle that broke out behind church,
an unanticipated shove
when he asked his father for the car keys
because of incense left burning in his closet,
I'll pass on the gravy spilled on my mother's
mother's lace tablecloth as we sit
for the final round of family. Maybe I'll keep
the plastic votives, battery-operated
artificial flickers, and how they look when placed
inside a vase, something like the way my heart
would feel when I imagined baby Jesus
coming here to save us. Keep the Dollar Store
branches of silver-blue beads the color of winter night,
something to gaze upon willingly. I'll keep
the hand-carved doll brought out again this year,
my mother's gift to me when I was nine,
and the hollow wooden apple that opens
to reveal a tiny place setting for two.

**Come to the Table**

Hold close the locks of hair and baby teeth
as scrimshaw, talisman of the long-ago child
you surrendered to, nursed and powdered.
*Come to the table for oatmeal and fruit.*

Now he's a man among masses in Chicago,
avoiding eye contact and dog crap all day.
Weekends we plant traps for a village of ants
who've invaded, pour little pools of poison

in their paths. I never get bored watching
the survivors. The line starts outside,
a constant segmented river marching along
transparent trails. It's instinct.

And all the messes made from little on,
removing his own diaper while I chatted
on the phone, circle of brown footprints
over rental carpet. A rock tossed high

in the air, landing on his face with blood
and bits of nose bone. *Come to the table
and we'll wipe it up.* Take a skateboard
down an unknown winding road,

broken clavicle and foot. We cling to risk
out of habit or genetics, how I mop his floor,
find stamp-sized plastic bags under the couch,
cling to rage that steeps like loose tea.

Who spilled pot leaves on the floor,
stepped in heroin and panicked at the mess?
*Oh, come to the table where we'll work it out,
sip our tea, be civil.* Maybe we'll find

something sweet.

## Sherpa

Someone has to haul
all our crap up hill,
make appointments, cancel,
reschedule. Make excuses. Cover
when the son's face goes red and blotchy,
nose stuffs up. Or, more alarming,
he shakes in a warm shower,
shakes under the quilt, shakes
out the words *I'll be all right*
from a sheet white face gone angular,
then *I don't know*. Someone
calls 911, ignores the neighbors'
stares, fits herself into a side seat
in the ambulance, says the word *heroin*
out loud, holds the puke pan, admits

she's his mother. Someone sits
with a panicked patient now pacing
in wait for the psych consult, neuro,
clergy. Someone steps to the curb
outside the hospital to hail a cab
while the son gathers his bathrobe around him,
and shuffles to the door in slippers brought
from home. Someone calls the father,
says *yes cancel everything and come*
so we can sit and weep together and alone
and hang on, as if his life depends on it.

## Still Life with Plate of Pinecone or Fish
*After* Gourds *by Matisse*

Read the dark backdrop as celestial, the blue
as window. When we look inside the mind
a water pitcher floats beyond the play
of midnight and morning, or rests on a table,
if you see it that way, on a black table cloth.
Yet there remains the drifting French casserole,
not tuna noodle with a can of soup, like my mother
made back when Matisse was still painting.
My son is with me at the museum, I guess to please
his mom. But with him, I've learned, my assumptions
are often wrong. I thought he had bad allergies,
the way his nose sometimes looked red and larger
than I'd remembered. His uncle was both drunk
and drugged then dead. But this is different.
Matisse's gourds are long-stemmed, the better
to handle. And an orange glass sits at the center,
between black and blue, holding still,
filled with sweet wine. *I'm fine, I'll be fine,*
he says on the subway beside me between dozes,
unable to explain open windows or being caught
in the night sky, uncertain about flying casseroles
and saucers, still life with plate of pinecone or fish.

**Family Night at Rehab**

They are pasty and fidgeting,
not quite committed to sitting in chairs.

At this moment there's nothing to do
but be here in their heavy chains

drinking weak coffee. We, the broken families,
drive for hours with sharpened pencils

to take notes, support our fading
loved ones. They're not dead yet

but not quite living, either, reeking
of cigarettes, unlaundered sweatshirts, greasy hair.

We're beyond slamming doors,
beyond shock and tears, beyond our savings,

hearing how their worlds' unknotted,
and the rough statistics, only twenty-five per cent

survive. We learn there's no predicting who.
We have nothing left to say to one another

(it's our second go around in rehab)
so he tries to make a joke about the checklist

of factors on the addiction handout:
family history, depression, anxiety,

peers using drugs, early drug use, risk takers.
*Look, mom, he says, I hit every one.*

## Elegy for my Son's Abandoned Music Career

What I miss most are the old jazz standards,
someone's heart stomped flat or shattered,
reminding me I'm not the only fool
for love. The tunes so pure I'd smell
spilled booze and smoke, when I visited
his college apartment on weekends, though
there was none of that as he practiced,
only mysterious plastic bags the size
of postage stamps, highs and lows
confounding me, a perfect score or none at all,
panic before each gig or school performance.

I'd sway to the music out of sight
so as not to embarrass myself
or distract him from fingering the strings,
coaxing chromatic movements, repeating notes
to build melodic tension. The tension
was immense—one day he's okay,
the next he's sick in bed.

I miss the warped versions of these old songs,
thick black LP's from my father's jazz collection
left too long in a dank basement, and how
he'd have loved seeing my son's fingers
trained on patterns, hearing fresh interpretations.
He'd wonder, too, how the music disappeared
note by fading note, frayed strings and sheet music
yellowing in the attic, stylus stuck and skipping.

# Section 3

**Scenes from an American Drama**

**Characters:** Mother of client. Therapist. Client.

**Scene One**

Stage directions: *Middle aged woman speaking to audience from behind the steering wheel of her Audi.*

MOTHER:

When I drive him to his therapist, he asks me to wait in the car. (His beater car off limits since he lost it one night in the city.)

The building would never be featured in Chicago's architectural tour, its rectangular shape, the ugly brick and tiny high windows could be a substitute for a jail or an elementary school in the city. If I were a mouse at their meeting, or a centipede, a silverfish, a daddy long legs spider, okay, even a cockroach, this is what I might overhear.

*This is what the characters are thinking.*

**Scene Two**

Stage directions: *Female therapist in drab professional clothes sitting behind a desk. Client sits on a desk chair with wheels, wearing blue jeans and a tee shirt. He fidgets and rolls around as he replies to questions.*

THERAPIST: So how's it going today?

*Two weeks out of hospital. I see dark circles under his eyes.*

CLIENT: I'm doing pretty well right now, I think.

*Nothing bothers me like therapy.*

THERAPIST: Your physical symptoms?

CLIENT: Fine.

*It's so chilly in this barren room.*

THERAPIST: Have you been to any AA meetings?

CLIENT: I wish there were a meeting close to me.

*I'm never going back to one of those. Middle-aged alcoholic women from Lake Forest don't get me.*

THERAPIST: What do you do to relax?

*Other than pot and heroin.*

CLIENT: I'm looking for a yoga class right now. My mother bought me a new yoga mat.

*Which I'll never use.*

THERAPIST: There's a yoga class across the street from here. Monday, I think.

*I'll have to get a ride for him I guess. His mother isn't living here full time.*

CLIENT: I need to practice for my gig that day.

*I can't see how those moves would help me now.*

THERAPIST: How's the music coming?

*His lame excuse again.*

CLIENT: Excellent!

*I probably won't feel so good next week. Unless I score. But I'm not planning to.*

THERAPIST: Anything else that I should know?

*I need to get my nails done pretty soon.*

CLIENT: I want to learn to meditate as well.

*Twenty minutes must be up by now.*

THERAPIST: Schedule another visit with me on your way out.

*If you can remember to.*

CLIENT: Sure thing.

*I don't want to see her any more. It doesn't fucking help.*

**Scene Three**

*Mother and client converse in mother's car.*

MOTHER: How'd it go?

SON: Pretty well.

**Scene Four:** Closing Monologue.

Stage directions: *After the client leaves his therapist's office, the therapist turns to the audience. Large, framed placards appear as wall hangings. Directions from a seed packet are printed on the placards. She reads them to the audience, pausing after each to deliver her comments.*

*Plant in early spring. Full sun.*

THERAPIST: Because spring in these parts comes late and lasts about two days (May 30 and 31st) I long to be among living things, growing things. I start seedlings in my office between appointments. The instructions on the seed packet read: Plant in early spring. Full sun.

There's a sour scent that surrounds my clients, addicts all. I'm glad I never had one. A child.

When is early spring? It's April first and snowing. Full sun seems a long way off.

*Sow in average soil*

THERAPIST: That's what we have here in the Midwest: plenty of average. It's an attitude that shouts, or, rather, whispers, we are average here. Hold to that.

Don't put yourself above anyone else.

*Firm lightly*

THERAPIST: Maybe this is where parents go wrong. How lightly to firm seedlings, off-sprouts, children? Maybe parents never read far enough in the instructions.

Trust, instead, to follow their hearts.

*Keep evenly moist*

THERAPIST: As if anything can be "kept." Kept evenly. One thing we know: the seedlings will emerge somehow. Even in average soil. Even in poor.

# E Mail

*From: Charles Le Claire, Lead Counselor*
*To: Vanessa Aublanc*
*Subject: Rough week at the Center*

Hey, Vanessa,
Charles here. Sorry to have been out of touch the last week or so. I did mean to call you sooner, sweetie, but an e-mail will have to do for now.

It's been a rotten week at the Center. On Monday I interviewed a prospective client for our live-in program. He came with his mother, a gal in her late fifties with a hippie sort of attitude about her: long peace sign earrings, jeans and a sweater that has seen better days. I may have detected patchouli on her. I will say that she shows concern: she has those blue-black circles under her eyes, and bags as well.

Instead of taking my advice and placing the kid in our live-in unit, she's talking about moving down here from Podunk Wisconsin to live with the junkie lad so that he can resume taking college course work. He's supposedly a musician, but if he doesn't shake this problem, he'll be a dead duck before graduation. They claim that his psychiatrist back in Wisco, AKA "slack-jaw county," recommends that he focus on his music and return to school.

So I accept him into our outpatient program. The first night he's here, we do a routine urine test, and the results are staggering: he's apparently ingested whatever he could get his hands on over the weekend back home. And he drove himself over here. I had to call Mrs. Stoney and give her the news. She seemed flabbergasted that her baby would (still, or again) do such a thing, but she did agree to take a cab to retrieve him.

Tuesday was family night, and you won't believe (wait till I tell you) what happened.

## Mrs. Stoney's Journal

The address indicates a building with an old stone façade. It was once a private home. I find parking, not too far away in this neighborhood of brownstones. The snow is mixing with sleet, and I take care not to slip. I'm buzzed in at the door by an invisible power. No one else in view, so I wait in a room that might have been the parlor. The furniture is ornate: a sofa and love seat, wooden legs, rich, paisley fabric—I think they call chintz. Table lamps give off soft, warm light. The large fireplace mantel is festooned with fresh pine boughs and red velvet ribbons: Christmas is not far away. In case we have to talk about things in the meeting, I've passed on the magazines with shiny covers, and make a list.

First time in Cook County jail (where being handsome holds no advantage)
Finding attorney #1
First court appearance
Driving around Chicago, searching for his car
First car accident
First ambulance ride
First trip to the ER
1,241 panic attacks, as judged by phone calls home (Do you think I'll be late for work? Do you think my shirt is pressed well enough? Why did I take this job? I have a performance tonight and I'm not prepared.)
First outpatient program
Thanksgiving from hell
Family meetings
Emptying home of any alcohol
Trips to psychologist, Milwaukee
Trips to psychiatrist, Milwaukee
First in-patient rehab
Trips to psychologist, Chicago
Trips to psychiatrist, Chicago
Finding attorney #2 (#1 didn't call back)
Sleepless nights (365 per year for four years)
Panic at the sound of the phone
Family night, family night, family night
Funeral for brother, dead from addiction
Funeral for cousin #1, dead from addiction
Funeral for cousin #2, dead from addiction
Janelle's alcoholism

## Another Family Night

A counselor appears. I recognize him from our intake interview. He's wearing gabardine slacks, perfectly tailored, Allen Edmond loafers, a maroon cashmere vee neck sweater over crisp white oxford shirt. Maybe it's his hair that gives him a striking resemblance to Alec Baldwin's character in 30 Rock. His head has that confident tilt. He calls himself Charles LeClaire, but I'd like to call him "Chuck." Behind him, a string of ordinary people. They're walking away from the parlor, down a hall and I assume Family Night is about to begin. The posh building does little to hide the awful truth: we're here to confront the nasty antics of our loved ones.

Under fluorescent lights, one or two of the clients drift in. Acrid cigarette smoke embedded in their clothing and hair, from their break between group session and this meeting. I haven't yet sat down when another rushes in. "Someone's having a seizure on the sidewalk."

I follow the others outside, feeling numb. He's lying in the snow. He stares blankly out from somewhere, at the night sky, with a look that says he doesn't recognize what's happening. Now I know what the cliché means: like a deer in headlights. I cup his head to protect it from the snowy shush. His beard is thin, almost blond, his light brown curls frame a handsome face, a roman nose at the center.

"Do you know him?" someone asks. I nod and hold his head in my hands until the paramedics arrive.

"Lucky to be alive," they say.

## Welcome to the ER

He's on a gurney in the common area. Uniformed people rushing about. My face feels like granite: the ambulance ride did little to calm me. I'm in panic mode, and wonder if this stone-faced façade covers my fear. ER workers don't like fear—they will not acknowledge it, maybe to remain calm themselves, pretend not to feel it. We wait in the hallway for a room. He vomits all over his clothes, so I grab a nearby basin. Finally a nurse appears. She's wearing a smock with little pink hearts and earrings in the shape of crosses. Her name tag says, "Nanci." I know this type, and imagine what her notes reveal.

*Nanci's nursing notes, employing the standard SOAP charting.*

Subjective: Mother states he uses heroin. Patient unable to give a history. Fellow junkies supposedly observed patient having a seizure.

Objective: Patient has shaking chills and is vomiting. Mother's cheeks are flush, and she's looking down at her feet.

Assessment: Likely heroin addiction and overdose. (Junkie. No wonder the mother feels shame. Jack and I will not make the same mistake. Already at four, our son Jason understands consequences, how they're very unpleasant. Kids are like seedlings: you have to shape them. My dad always said "To grow a tree straight, you have to stake it." My son will be staked by the crucifix of Jesus.)

Plan: Run every test available, including spinal tap (it scares the shit out of them). Psych consult. Neurology consult. No opiates or other meds. (Let him detox on the ward for a couple of days.) The neurologist will say "You're lucky to be alive."

I pace the hallways, not wanting to watch withdrawal, not wanting to take that kind of abuse. Again.

**Rock Bottom**

Where is rock bottom, anyway?
We're waiting. He looks
under the subway, between tracks,
even in another fluorescent meeting
of smoke embedded stories, as if listening
could thread his way back.
Might he find it in his mitochondria,
a single cell under micrcoscope,
dank basements, filthy apartment sofas,
alone, some friends are missing,
comfort uninhabitable with pressure building like
roiling volcanic magna,
just enough cash for a one-way
ticket home in hand, hand in hand
in everything. Fears what he will not become:
recovering.

## All Rise, Court is Now in Session

Let the record show that I'm an expensive attorney.

Let the record show that my client is wearing a dark suit and tie unlike any other person in the room, except his father and me.

Let the record show that no one else in the courtroom has hired private counsel.

Let the record show that the honorable Madame Judge flashed a smile at my client.

Let the record show that my client's parents are both professionals, and that they are both here with him today, by his side, all the way from Wisconsin.

Let the record show that my client is the only white boy in court today.

Let the record show that the judge said to my client "you're lucky to be alive."

Let the record show that one boy, about seventeen, is alone in court today, without parents or counsel or a suit.

Let the record show my client is completing a degree from the Chicago Center for Performing Arts and has a bright future serving tables.

Let the record show that he is the only person whose case is being dismissed today.

Let the record show that he cannot spend more than a weekend at his home in Wisconsin because the surroundings and former friends call him back to his junkie self.

Let the record show that my client will leave the country after graduation.

Let the record show he'll choose to live in a third world country with little infrastructure, poor plumbing and no health care, feeling lucky, for now, to be alive.

# Epilogue

### The Road Finally Taken
*After Robert Frost*

Two roads diverged in his ravaged life
and knowing he could not travel both
and be alive, long he stood
at a broken door

on the south side, far from the tidy
stone walls of university,
from florescent lights
of rehab, from the family home

reading again his brother's text
*Come with me to a village*
*we've never seen, to people*
*we've never met*

then answered *yes*
and hailed a cab
and that has made
all the difference.

**Crumbs**

Like you, child, I might have walked
for miles down the gravel road along the creek
by my childhood home to nibble
a cornice of rooftop, lick icing mortar,
risk catching my tongue on a crevice
of crystallized sugar and waited
for the slice, that flat taste of blood to flow.

Or followed Alice and the mushrooms—
that's a sweet road, too, falling like soft bread,
squished down, then stretching again,
filling her white tights like a fat sausage,
as if that—adding all the scraps—
would be the way back home.

Imagine that witch's backside,
pushing and shoving her into
a little box of hell. Even old, lean bones
show direction when they land
like the hands of a compass.

If home is a place to imagine,
if size isn't really the point,
then the porridge is equally salty
from any bowl, mama's or dad's.
And bed could be any warm corner
like a ham slice, so snug on a roll.

Keep that snack in a napkin or kerchief—
don't waste crumbs coming back.

## Asteroid

If it's true that rocks bear calcified stardust,
he spends his days hoisting stars
from the rugged Guatemalan land.

Until his bright ripening he wandered
mind-numbing streets, as lost as in a maze
carved from drying corn stalks.

Now he mines the land, grabbing avocados
where they fall, snatching tomatoes from their
heavy limbs, storing jocote for jam and wine.

Anyone who risks plunging into the dark,
willing to mix animal dung and insect casings,
could be rewarded. Anyone who breathes today

can gather pollen or starlight or stones.

## Zenith

In Guatemala Orion sits strait overhead,
more saucepan than belt and sword.
On this land of ancient Mayan
he mines rocks, still thinking
of that pattern found in childhood
from tracing his body. A man could trip
over his fortune, recognize the celestial
in the landscape under foot, mark
where stones mimic stars. Here, volcanoes
form new land and mysteries lie in the deep
bed of Lake Atitlan a thousand feet below.

In the village of San Marcos all fracture
and fault, all body memory of escarpment
recedes. So unlike shallow Lake Winnebago
of his childhood, a marshy bed of pond weed,
so unlike turbulent Lake Michigan
whose shipwrecks and shoreline meet Chicago,
that butcher city, mecca of lost souls.
San Marcos, village of his own discovery,
landscape for the soul, the name as soothing
as a Spanish lullaby, *A la puerta del cielo,*
at the door to the sky.

**Viento**

Someone practices trumpet in barrio one
afternoons when whitecaps race like leaping fish
across Lake Atitlan. It seems an unlikely time
for a wind instrument, when most people gather
twigs and branches for cooking their evening meal.

As smoke settles over the village, the trumpeter
blows air through closed lips until a wave
vibration begins. All I know of trumpet is jazz
which is not hot in San Marcos. Hot here is direct
sun from morning till dusk unless you find shade

or a breeze. Hot here are windchimes played
by gusts. Hot is coffee, chocolate, homemade sauce.
Early evening a guitarist strums simple chords
for his neighbors, maybe a church thing,
and they sing, often off key, and clap hands.

Later yet, after sundown, mangy travelers gather
at a hostel on the lake, drum bongos
and imagine they make good music that stirs souls.
But it sounds, to this North American ear, like the natives
are restless. Except they don't appear that way,

the locals. Not the kind of people to challenge,
and everyone you meet looks you directly
in the eye, and even when carrying fruit
in heavy baskets on their heads or bags
of rocks uphill, stops to say *"Buenos Dias."*

Readers Guide:
1. Why does the mother, in the opening poem, apologize for having had a c-section?
2. What warning signs were there indicating Star Boy was struggling with addiction? (may promote identification of warning signs in the reader's own life)
3. Do you see any places where the mother appears removed? Annoyed? Angry?
4. Could the mother have done anything differently to prevent son's addiction? (this question promotes analysis of the nature vs nurture aspect of addiction)
5. Anyone noticeably absent? What affect could the absence have had in this story?
6. Star Boy appeared disinterested and disengaged during the therapy session. What could the therapist have said and/or done differently to improve his motivation for treatment?
7. What stigmatizing statements are noted in the book? How could these types of beliefs affect the way healthcare providers treated Star Boy? What impact could that have had on Star Boy?
8. Are there any other ways the mother could have done to support her son's addiction recovery?
9. What are some examples of emotionally supporting vs. enabling of a loved ones' addiction?
10. Is there a line or a setting you can relate to?


End of Book Recommendation:
If you or a loved one is struggling with addiction, there are people waiting to help: AODA support services include National Helplines, AA, NA, Al-Anon, Nar-Anon, NAMI, National Suicide Hotline, the HOPELINE.

www.ingramcontent.com/pod-product-compliance
Lightning Source LLC
LaVergne TN
LVHW040116080426
835507LV00041B/1145